Mankato, MN ; Crestwood House. c1986.

Series title: working dogs.

MILITARY DOGS

BY PHYLLIS RAYBIN EMERT

EDITED BY DR. HOWARD SCHROEDER
Professor in Reading and Language Arts
Dept. of Elementary Education
Mankato State University

PRODUCED & DESIGNED BY
BAKER STREET PRODUCTIONS

CRESTWOOD HOUSE

LIBRARY OF CONGRESS CATALOGING IN PUBLICATION DATA
Emert, Phyllis Raybin.
  Military dogs.

  (Working dogs)
  SUMMARY: Discusses the use of dogs in military campaigns throughout history describing the breeds most often used and how they are
trained.
  1. Dogs, War use--Juvenile literature. (1. Dogs--War use. 2. Working
dogs. 3. Dogs) I. Schroeder, Howard. II. Title. III. Series
UH100.E43   1985   355.8   85-17488
ISBN 0-89686-286-0 (lib. bdg.)

International Standard	Library of Congress
Book Number:	Catalog Card Number:
Library Binding 0-89686-286-0	85-17488

ILLUSTRATION CREDITS

Peter Hornby: Cover, 16, 19, 24-25, 35, 37, 42
U.S. Army Photo: 4, 26, 32
Signal Corps Photo: 7
U.S. Marine Corps Photo: 8, 12
U.S. Defense Dept. Photo: 11
U.S. Air Force Photo: 15, 21, 29, 38, 45
P.R. Emert: 22

CRESTWOOD HOUSE
Hwy. 66 South, Box 3427
Mankato, MN 56002-3427

Table of contents

The author wishes to acknowledge the following people and organizations without whose help and cooperation this book would not have been possible:

Ernest V. Paz, Program Director, Department of Defense Dog Center, Lackland Air Force Base, Texas;

Hildegarde Brown, Public Relations, Department of Defense Dog Center, Lackland Air Force Base, Texas;

Danny J. Crawford, Head, Reference Section, History and Museums Division, Department of the Navy, Headquarters United States Marine Corps, Washington, D.C.;

Lt. Colonel Robert Gibson, United States Air Force, Director, Public Affairs, Lackland Air Force Base, Texas;

Capt. Virginia A. Allen, United States Army, Special Activities and Media Initiatives Branch, Department of the Army, Washington, D.C.;

United States Army AG Publications Center, Baltimore, Maryland.

Special thanks to M.W. and Y. Raybin.

1.
Chips and Caesar

It was July 10, 1943. The United States was at war with Germany, Italy, and Japan. A dog named Chips stood alertly next to his handler, Private John Rowell. ''Easy, Chips,'' said Rowell. He patted the big dog's head. They were part of the invasion force waiting to land on the beach at Sicily, an island off the coast of Italy.

Chips was a husky-German shepherd-collie mix. He

Chips, the World War II dog hero, in a 1943 photo.

was a member of the K-9 (canine) Corps in the American Seventh Army. Three thousand ships carried soldiers, guns, and tanks to land on the beaches of Sicily. American, Canadian, and British troops were all taking part in the invasion.

The story of Chips, though, begins in Pleasantville, New York. He lived with the Edward Wren family. As a pup, Chips played with the Wrens', two little girls. He sometimes went to school with nine-year-old Gail, the oldest girl.

He was a strong, smart pup. Chips was also a good guard dog. He protected the family. But he had one problem. He snapped at strangers. He even bit the garbageman.

At the start of World War II, Mr. Wren told his wife and daughters, "Chips is a born fighter. I understand that the Army needs dogs like him to help win the war." The family agreed.

Chips joined the Army in 1942. He was trained as a sentry (guard) and attack dog at the War Dog Training Center in Front Royal, Virginia. There he met his handler, Private Rowell. Chips was a member of the first War Dog Detachment to be sent from America to Africa. He sailed aboard a troop ship.

Chips' first battle was in French Morroco. Bullets were flying as the soldiers landed on the beach. Bombs were dropping. Rowell quickly dug a foxhole for protection. Chips dug one, too, as he had been taught to do.

At night, enemy troops sometimes killed human sentries in the dark. Others would stab soldiers while they slept. But no sentries or soldiers were killed in units with K-9 Corps dogs. The dogs were trained to alert the soldiers to the enemy.

Now Chips and Rowell were about to fight again in Sicily. "It's time, boy," said Rowell. They moved off the landing craft and onto the beach with the other soldiers. Chips and Rowell moved slowly forward in the darkness of the early morning.

Suddenly, bullets began spraying the area. "Take cover," yelled an officer. The soldiers flattened themselves in the sand. Chips began whining and barking. He saw that the bullets were coming from a hut near the beach.

Chips didn't wait for orders from Rowell. Showing his teeth, Chips charged the hut. Bullets flew all around the big dog as he ran inside.

Shrieks and growls cut through the air. "I saw one Italian soldier come out the door with Chips at his throat," said Private Rowell. "I called him off before he could kill the man." Three other soldiers came out with their hands up. Chips had powder burns and a small head wound.

Later, Chips alerted his unit to ten more enemy soldiers sneaking down the beach. Rowell captured them all.

Chips saved many American lives that morning. Officers recommended him for three medals—a

Distinguished Service Cross, the Purple Heart, and the Silver Star for bravery. But the War Department decided that medals could only be given to people, not animals. Chips never received the awards. However, news of his bravery appeared in newspapers all across the United States, and Chips became famous.

Chips was also part of the heavy fighting in the Battle of Salerno in Italy. During that battle he met General Dwight D. Eisenhower. The General bent over to pet the well-known hero. But only a dog's handler is allowed to do that. So Chips bit him! General Eisenhower became President of the United States in 1952.

Chips meets General Eisenhower.

Chips went on to fight all over Italy, France, and Germany, in the Rhineland, Central Europe, and with the Military Police. Unofficially, his unit awarded him eight battle stars. They gave him one star for each of the eight battles in which he took part.

A few months after Chips hit the beach at Sicily, another dog went into combat. This dog, named Caesar, was in the South Pacific, where U.S. Marines were fighting the Japanese. They were in the jungles of Bougainville, one of the Solomon Islands. Caesar, a German shepherd, was a messenger dog.

Caesar and handler, John Kleeman.

It's many thousand miles from New York City to Bougainville. But that's how far Caesar had come. He belonged to the Max Glazer family. The little shepherd pup grew up to be a very large, black and grey dog. Caesar was very smart. Caesar was strong, too. He could easily jump over a park bench.

The big shepherd was well-known in his New York neighborhood. Everyday, he would carry things home from the grocery store to Mrs. Glazer. One of the Glazer's sons would say to the dog, "Take it to Mom." Off went Caesar with a package of meat or a loaf of bread in his mouth.

After the War started, all three Glazer boys went into the service. The family agreed that Caesar should also help his country.

The Army trained Caesar to be a messenger. Then he was transferred to Camp LeJeune, the Marine training camp in North Carolina. Caesar met his new handlers there—Private First Class John Kleeman and Private First Class Rufus Mayo. Kleeman and Mayo got very attached to the big, shepherd dog. When Mayo wrote home, he always had Caesar make a paw print on the bottom of the letter.

The Marines sailed from San Diego, California, in June, 1943. By November, they were in heavy combat in the jungles of Bougainville.

Soon after arriving, Caesar and Mayo were assigned to a company on the front lines. Walkie-talkie radios didn't work in the thick jungle. Telephone lines between the command post and the company had been cut by the enemy. "You're the only way we can get our messages through, Caesar," said Mayo to the big dog. "Report!"

Off Caesar went to carry the messages to Kleeman at the command post. Caesar ran fast, dodging bullets from Japanese snipers. Caesar went back and forth nine times. For two days and two nights, he was the only link between the Marines and headquarters.

During the second night, Mayo and Caesar settled down to sleep in their foxhole. After a time, Caesar heard a noise. The dog woke up Mayo. Mayo opened his eyes in time to see a grenade land at his feet. He grabbed the small bomb and threw it. The grenade exploded. "That was a close one, Caesar," said Mayo. "You saved our lives." The next morning, Mayo found eight enemy bodies. They were killed by the grenade that was meant for him and Caesar.

Before dawn on the third day, the Japanese began to attack. An enemy soldier was trying to sneak up on Mayo in the foxhole. Caesar leaped out and raced toward the man. Mayo shouted at the dog. "Come, Caesar, come!" Caesar wasn't trained to be an attack dog.

The big shepherd obeyed his master's command. As he turned back to Mayo, the enemy shot him twice. One bullet entered his shoulder. The other hit him in the back. When the enemy attack was over, Mayo found Caesar back at the command post. The bleeding dog way to Kleeman. Caesar was the first Marine dog to be injured in battle.

Mayo hugged him. "You'll make it, boy. You're going to be all right," he said, close to tears. Some other Marines chopped down some bamboo poles. Then they tied them together and attached a blanket. It was a stretcher for Caesar. Mayo and Kleeman carried the wounded dog to a first aid station.

The wounded Caesar is taken to a first aid station by his handlers.

The doctor took out one of the bullets. "The shoulder bullet is too near Caesar's heart to operate," he told the worried Marines. "But he still might pull through."

As time passed, Caesar got better. The rest of the company asked for news about him each day. They gave him their best food and a lot of attention. After three weeks, Caesar was well enough to go back to his company!

A Marine Headquarters Bulletin stated in 1944, "Caesar of Bougainville would be wearing the Purple Heart if medals were officially awarded to animal warriors." A letter from the Marine Corps Commandant was sent to the Glazer family praising the German shepherd.

To this day, Chips and Caesar are remembered as two of the bravest and best military dogs of World War II.

Caesar recovered well enough to go back to his company.

2.

Ancient armies used dogs

Armies have used dogs throughout history. The ancient Assyrians, Persians, and Babylonians used large, strong dogs with spiked collars to attack the enemy. These dogs were called mastiffs.

The Romans were the first to have regular war-dog units. Their dogs wore armor and spiked collars. The dogs attacked the legs of the enemy. This forced the enemy to lower their shields, leaving their bodies open to attack by soldiers.

The Spaniards brought attack dogs to the New World in 1494. Some of these dogs were so good at their jobs that they were paid a salary!

Napoleon, the French Emperor, used sentry dogs to give warning of attackers. Benjamin Franklin wanted to train ''large and fierce soldier dogs'' to protect the American colonists. But it was never done. It wasn't until the Civil War that Americans first used dogs in combat, as messengers.

In World War I, the Germans trained thirty thousand dogs for messenger and ambulance work. French and Belgian forces used dogs as sentries and messengers.

The Americans had no dog units.

In the Second World War, dogs were used by both sides. They saved many soldiers from surprise attacks. The Germans trained more than 200,000 dogs for different duties during the war. The Russians used Samoyeds in dog sled teams. They carried soldiers into battle and located the wounded. The British, French, and Japanese also used war dogs.

In July of 1942, the United States opened the first American War Dog Training Center in Front Royal, Virginia. Later, four other training centers were opened.

The K-9 Corps

At first, American dogs were trained as sentries. After a time, they were also trained as sleddogs, scouts, messengers, and wire-laying dogs. These American war dogs were known as "K-9's." A civilian agency called Dogs for Defense supplied dogs to the military free of charge. The dogs were donated by volunteers all across the country.

The Marines trained their dogs at Camp LeJeune, North Carolina. They were called "Devildogs." Devildogs were the first, large, dog unit to fight against the enemy.

Hundreds of K-9 Corps members fought in North Africa, Europe, and the Pacific against the Germans, Italians, and Japanese. More than nine thousand dogs were on sentry duty and beach patrol on U.S. coasts.

They also helped protect military bases and factories in America from spies and enemy agents.

In the early 1950's, sentry and scout dogs were used by U.S. forces fighting in Korea. In 1952 and 1953, the U.S. Air Force opened sentry-dog schools in Japan and then Germany.

Since 1958, the U.S. Department of Defense (DOD) has trained their dogs at Lackland Air Force Base, Texas. Dogs are trained here at Lackland for all branches of the U.S. armed services.

Nemo, the first dog hero of the Vietnam War, lost an eye in combat.

In the Vietnam War, 1965 to 1973, dogs were used as scouts, sentries, mine and tunnel detectors, and water dogs. (See Part 4.) The scout dogs were trained at Fort Benning, Georgia. The dogs practiced in the fields and swamps of Georgia, which are very similar to land areas in Vietnam. Most of the other dogs were trained at Lackland. Since 1971, U.S. military dogs have also been trained to detect drugs and explosives.

Today, patrol dogs are used for routine sentry duty. They're taught to scout, track, search, and guard military areas. Some are trained to search out drugs or bombs. The DOD Dog Center even supplies dogs for U.S. Federal agencies such as the Secret Service, the Federal Aviation Administration, and the Department of Agriculture.

This patrol dog is guarding an air base.

3.

Requirements

Military dogs must be smart and dependable. They should be alert and easy to train. Their actions must be predictable. The handler must always know how the dog will behave in certain situations.

Military dogs need strength and the will to work. They need to work in all kinds of weather. The dog must have a good sense of smell and good hearing in order to help soldiers.

Dogs in the military must be large enough to fight an attacker, if necessary. They shouldn't be shy or afraid of noises.

Dogs are donated or bought by the Department of Defense Dog Center from American civilians. The Dog Center pays up to $400.00 (U.S.) for each dog. They must be between one and four years of age, and can either be male or female. Dogs should be at least twenty-two inches (56.4 cm) tall at the shoulder and weigh fifty-five pounds (25 kg) or more. The dogs must be in excellent health.

Thirty-two different breeds were accepted for service at the start of World War II. As the years passed, many breeds did not fit into the military-dog program. By late 1944, the U.S. Army only accepted five breeds of dogs.

They were German shepherds, Belgian sheepdogs, Doberman pinschers, collies and giant schnauzers.

Since then, different dogs have been used at different times. It depends on American military involvement around the world. Today, only working dogs like the Bouvier des Flandres, giant schnauzers, and Belgian Malinois are recruited. In past years, German short-haired pointers, Labrador retrievers, and golden retrievers have been used.

Over the years, three breeds of dogs have been used most often by the armed forces. Doberman pinschers were popular military dogs in World War II. For a time, they were the official dog of the Marine Corps. The Marines felt that the short-haired Doberman adapted easier to the tropical jungles of the South Pacific than other breeds.

Today, most people feel that the German shepherd is the best all-around military dog. The German shepherd has been used by the armed forces more than any other breed. Rottweilers are the other favorite breed used by the military.

Doberman pinschers

Louis Doberman lived in Thuringen, Germany in the 1870's. He was attacked and robbed many times while walking at night. Doberman decided to breed a dog for his own protection.

The Doberman pinscher.

He started by crossing a Rottweiler with a German shepherd. Then he bred that dog with a Manchester terrier, a greyhound, and a Weimaraner. By the 1890's, he had the guard dog he wanted. Named after himself, Doberman added the German word for terrier, "pinscher."

Doberman pinschers are powerful fighters. Their bodies are very strong. They are fast, alert, sleek, and sturdy dogs. They're quick to learn and have a good sense of smell.

Pinschers are full of energy and unafraid. They are fierce-looking dogs. Over the years, careless breeding has produced some Dobermans with uneven tempers. Some of these dogs are too nervous and hard to control. But, when bred properly, the Doberman pinscher is one of the easiest breeds to train and control.

Dobermans have hard, short, and smooth coats. The ears are cut to points. Its tail is clipped short. These dogs are black, red, tan, or brown in color. Reddish-brown markings are over each eye. These markings are also on the muzzle (face), throat, chest, legs, and feet.

Males are twenty-six to twenty-eight inches (66.7 - 71.8 cm) tall at the shoulder. Females are twenty-four to twenty-six inches (61.5 - 66.7 cm) tall. Doberman pinschers weigh between fifty and seventy-five pounds (22.7 - 34.1 kg).

German shepherds

The shepherd dogs of Germany were trained to herd and protect flocks of cattle and sheep. They were smart and dependable dogs. In 1887, Captain Max von Stephanitz helped start the German Shepherd Dog Club of Germany. Von Stephanitz wanted to make the shepherd dog a valuable working partner for all people. He tried to breed dogs that were smart and had an even temper. Other breeders soon followed his guidelines. They produced working dogs of high quality.

The Germans used shepherd dogs in World War I. After the war, returning soldiers brought them home to England and America. They became very popular. Two German shepherds, Rin Tin Tin and Strongheart, became famous movie stars.

Demand for shepherd dogs grew. Large numbers of them were produced. But the breeders became careless. Many dogs were too nervous. Some were even vicious. Their popularity dropped.

Yet, German breeders never stopped producing high-quality dogs. Today, the descendants of these dogs work at many different jobs, helping people.

German breeders produced the finest German shepherds.

The German shepherd has a double coat of medium length. The rough coat is thick and straight. It lies close to the body.

Shepherds are loyal and friendly. But they're also powerful fighters. Most German shepherds are brown, tan, black or grey in color. Some are white.

Females are twenty-two to twenty-four inches (56.4 - 61.5 cm) tall at the shoulder. They weigh sixty to seventy pounds (27.3 - 31.8 kg). Males are twenty-four to twenty-six inches (61.5 - 66.7 cm) tall and weigh seventy-five to eighty-five pounds (34.1 - 38.6 kg).

Rottweilers

The Rottweiler is related to the cattle dog of the Roman Empire of long ago. The Romans used the dogs

Rottweilers are brave and fierce fighters.

to drive cattle over the Alps into Central Europe. After a time, the Romans left. The dogs stayed behind in Germany, nineteen hundred years ago. They were named after the town of Rottweil.

In Germany, the Rottweiler was used to drive herds of cattle to market. Some pulled carts. Others guarded people. Merchants would tie their money bags around the dog's neck. Thieves were afraid to go near the dogs and rob them.

In the late 1800's, a German law stopped the use of dogs for cattle-driving. The Rottweilers were then used more as working dogs. They pulled heavy loads and were trained in military and police work.

Rottweilers are obedient, calm, and even-tempered. They are very strong and muscular. As guard dogs, they can be brave and fierce fighters. But they're also very devoted to their masters.

The coats of Rottweilers are short, rough, and lie flat. The tail is cut very short. These dogs are mostly black in color. Tan or reddish-brown markings are on the muzzle, cheeks, chest, legs, and over both eyes. Rottweilers are twenty-two to twenty-seven inches (56.4 - 69.2 cm) tall at the shoulder. They weigh seventy-five to one hundred pounds (34.1 - 45.5 kg).

On guard at a military air base.

4.

Basic training — World War II

Most U.S. military training for dogs in World War II lasted twelve to fourteen weeks. Sentry dog training took eight weeks. Basic (or beginning) training was similar for all the branches of the armed services. The dogs were shipped in crates to dog-training centers. A record book was started for every K-9 Corps dog. All

A K-9 named Pal at Camp Adair, Oregon, in 1943.

important information was listed in the record book.

A complete physical examination was given to each new dog "soldier." The dog's serial number was tatooed on his left ear, flank (side), or belly. Each animal had its own kennel. Clean, fresh straw was placed on the floor. Marine kennels had wooden decks with a twenty-by-fifty foot concrete runway.

All dogs were groomed each day. They were taught never to accept food from anyone but their handlers. Dogs ate horsemeat mixed with cornmeal, and regular dog food.

Handlers

New dogs spent the first three weeks apart from the other dogs, in "isolation." This was done to make sure they were free from disease. During this time, they met their handlers. Most handlers were military volunteers who loved dogs.

The handlers learned about the care, feeding, and training of war dogs. Most K-9's were matched with one handler to form a "dog unit." The Marines assigned two handlers to each dog. Messenger and wire-laying dogs were also assigned two handlers.

After isolation, the dog and its handler went to classes together. The classes were taught by experienced dog trainers. Dogs worked a total of five hours each day, six days a week.

Obedience training

All military dogs were trained first in basic obedience. The dogs were taught to "heel" (walk alongside the handler) on and off the leash. The dogs then learned to "sit," "get down," and "stay" on command. They learned to "come" when called. Many dogs were also taught to "crawl," "drop," or "take cover." At the command "up," dogs learned to jump and climb over walls.

The dogs were taught to crawl through small openings in barbed-wire fences. They rode in military vehicles. The dogs crossed streams and climbed fences. They went over ramps and across ditches. Most dogs enjoyed this part of the training. Patience and praise were always used by the handlers. Some dogs were taught to obey hand signals and silent whistles, as well as the handler's voice.

Battle noise

Dogs and handlers were exposed to all types of gunfire, land mines, and smoke screens. Getting used to battle noise was an important part of military training.

Dogs were first tested under small arms fire. After a time, they were exposed to seventy-five millimeter cannons. These large guns fired six or seven rounds at a time. The noise was very loud. Only the steadiest

This German shepherd is getting used to small arms fire.

dog would pass. The successful K-9 paid no attention to the sounds of weapons, no matter how loud. The dogs who couldn't adjust were sent home.

Advanced training

In advanced training, the dogs were taught the special jobs they would be doing in the war. Trainers and handlers decided which dog would be best for the job. Temperament, size, and intelligence were taken into account. Dogs were trained to be sentries, sentry-attack dogs, scouts, messengers, casualty dogs, wire-laying dogs, pack dogs, or sleddogs. The training for each job was different.

Sentry dogs & sentry-attack dogs

Most WWII K-9's were trained for sentry duty. They guarded more than five hundred defense plants, factories, military bases, and supply depots. The Coast Guard and Navy used sentry dogs to guard America's coastlines. Sometimes, these dogs wore leather boots to protect their feet while patrolling rocky beaches. The dogs worked mainly at night.

The sentry dog worked with a soldier on guard duty. The sentry dog gave warning and then located unseen people on command. The dogs were taught to work on a short leash. No one could surprise a sentry by hiding behind a building or some trees.

While on duty, the dog was given the command, "watch." The sentry K-9's used their excellent hearing and sense of smell to find people. If a dog detected someone, it alerted its handler. Some dogs alerted by growling quietly. Others alerted silently. The handler got to know the special way their dog alerted. Each one was different.

Some sentry dogs were also trained to attack off the leash. A handler ordered the dog to attack by saying, "get him." The dog was trained to attack the right arm (weapon arm) of the enemy. The command, "out," was used to stop the dog. These sentry-attack dogs were mainly used by the military police. Any move against the handler would cause the dog to attack on its own.

Scout dogs

The scout dog was trained to work on and off the leash. The scout gave silent warning of the enemy while on patrol. Some were able to detect enemy soldiers five hundred yards away. Marine scout dogs in the South Pacific saved many American lives.

On a leash, the dog alerted quietly like a sentry. Off the leash, the scout dog worked fifty to seventy-five feet (15.4 - 23.1 m) in front of the handler. The handler walked ahead of the patrol. The command "watch" was given to the dog. The K-9 would detect hidden enemies and alert the handler. Scouts were usually sent ahead on trails to detect ambushes. They were also used to explore huts and buildings.

Messengers

Messenger dogs were used when there was no other way of communication. They carried messages from

Handlers put a message pouch around the neck of a WWII messenger dog.

the front lines to the command post, and back again. The dogs were often under heavy gunfire.

Messenger dogs were strong and fast. The messages were carried in a pouch on the dog's collar. These dogs were always assigned to two handlers. When given the command "report" they ran from one handler (on patrol) to the other handler (at the command post). The dog was trained to run miles at a time.

Special jobs

Instead of carrying messages in a pouch, wire-laying dogs carried wire on a spindle for communication lines. The wire unwound as the dog ran from one handler to another. Casualty dogs helped the Medical Corps locate wounded soldiers when the command, "search," was given. The dogs used their sense of smell to find people. They would alert the handler, who followed the dog back to the wounded person.

Sleddogs rescued the wounded in bad weather, over rough ground. The dogs and sled were sometimes parachuted into snowy areas where planes could not land. Pack dogs carried first aid, supplies, and ammunition. A single pack dog could carry thirty pounds (13.6 kg) of supplies or weapons all day long.

Retraining after the war

After the war, dogs were retrained to be gentle, family pets. The dogs were taught that every person was a friend. They were handled and played with by many people.

Before being sent home, the dog had to pass a final test. The dog was walked by a building on a leash. A person jumped out suddenly, shouting and waving a sack. If the dog tried to make friends, it passed the test. About five percent of the war dogs that had been on active duty failed this test. They were too vicious to be retrained. With the consent of their owners, these dogs were put to sleep.

Most WWII K-9's were returned to their old owners. Others were kept by American soldiers, with the owner's permission. The rest were sold by the U.S. government to good homes.

Korea

In 1950, fighting broke out in Korea. Scout dogs saw much service there. They took part in hundreds of combat patrols. Sentry dogs were used by the Army and Air Force in Korea. They guarded military bases and supply areas.

Vietnam

The Vietnam War was different than any other. So was the training of military dogs.

Scout dogs were trained to take part in jungle combat. Their training lasted twelve weeks. Obedience was taught first. The dog learned hand and arm signals, and voice commands. Both daylight and night scouting was taught. The dogs relied on their excellent sense of smell.

Scout dogs alerted to either live or dead scents in Vietnam. A live scent was a human being. A dead scent

Scout dogs alerted to both live and dead scents in Vietnam.

could be anything else unusual. The handler learned to tell a live or dead scent by how excited the dog acted while alerting.

When K-9's alerted on patrol, the handler put up a hand to stop the patrol. Then the handler bent down behind the dog, stretching his arms out in the direction of the alert. This was done silently. The dog and handler moved to the back of the patrol. The other soldiers would then go in after the enemy.

In the early part of the war, scout dogs were trained to detect tunnels, mines, and booby traps. After several years, special dogs were trained for each of these duties.

Tunnel-detector dogs scented out the enemy in underground tunnels, holes, and caves. Mine dogs detected the smell of the mine or booby trap, or the scent of the person who planted it. The dog also noticed the change in the ground where it was buried. Dogs were trained to sit within two feet of the mine or trap. They were rewarded with food treats or praise.

Dogs were also trained to alert to trip wires. At first, the dog was allowed to go through the wire. This set off a small explosion, scaring the dog. Then it was corrected by the handler. After several practices, dogs learned to alert to the trip wire. They wouldn't cross it, but instead moved from one end of the wire to the other.

Water dogs alerted to the enemy who hid completely underwater. The enemy breathed through reeds that poked above the water's surface. Water dogs also detected enemy soldiers hidden in holes along the river-banks. The dogs detected the scent of the enemy from the small air holes or reeds they used for breathing!

These dogs were so successful that the Viet Cong enemy had orders to kill the dog first, and then the handler.

5.

The patrol dog

Today, patrol dogs are the standard working dog of the United States military services. They are a familiar sight at military bases. Sentry dogs are no longer trained by the military. They were too aggressive (ready to attack or fight) and unsafe around people.

Patrol dogs are a common sight at military bases today.

Patrol dogs are safe, on and off the leash. They are controlled by the handlers at all times. Patrol dogs attack, but only on command. They can be called back from an attack by voice command from the handler. This is called "controlled aggression."

Patrol dogs are used in almost any area of a military base, day and night. They're used for routine guard duty. They also search and find people in buildings and

A military dog is taught to attack a suspect in a buiding search.

open areas. They can track criminals or lost children by following scent trails. Patrol dogs with an excellent sense of smell are selected for drug and bomb-detector training.

Selecting military dogs

A dog must pass several tests before being chosen for today's military dog, training program. First, the dog is teased and annoyed by a stranger. If a dog has to be touched to make it pay attention, it's not selected. Dogs who back off or ignore the person are not chosen either. A dog that makes a move toward the stranger is selected for patrol dog training.

In the next test, the dog is put on a long leash. Seventy-five yards (69.2 m) from the dog, a person fires six blanks from a gun into the air. The dog is led by the handler closer to the gun as it is fired. By the time the last shot is fired, the dog must come within ten yards (9.2 m) of the gun. Dogs who are afraid of gunshot noises are not selected for military service.

The selected dogs are shipped to Lackland Air Force Base in Texas. The dogs are examined by a veterinarian. If the dogs are in good health, they are ready for basic training.

Handlers

All handlers are military-police volunteers who enjoy working with dogs. They have all passed a special dog-handler, training course. The handler feeds, grooms, plays with, and exercises the dog each day. In this way, the dog and handler form a close bond with each other.

A dog is assigned to only one handler. But the handler may be assigned more than one dog. The handler is always patient and firm with the dog during training.

Rewards and corrections

A dog is trained by 1) repeating the lesson, and 2) the use of rewards and corrections. When the dog is correct, it is rewarded. A dog is rewarded with spoken praise, petting, and sometimes food treats or toys.

If the dog is not correct, it doesn't get the reward. The handler will say, "no." If voice corrections don't work, the handler jerks on the leash. A loud "no," together with a quick jerk on the leash, will make it clear to the dog that it is not correct. Great force or pain is never used.

Basic obedience training

Dogs are usually trained for twenty minutes at a time. They then have a ten minute break. There may be several training sessions each day. The first part of basic training is obedience commands. Voice and hand commands are used together.

The basic command is "heel." The dog is trained to walk or sit at the left side of the handler. For the "sit" command, the dog sits beside the left leg of the handler. The dog is praised each time it obeys the commands correctly.

In the "down" position, the dog lays next to the handler. After the "stay" command, the dog must keep in position until another command is given. If the dog has trouble, the handler will gently push the animal into the correct position. After a time, the handler gives the obedience commands at a distance from the dog. Soon the dog will learn to obey commands from up to fifty feet away.

Each animal also goes through gunfire training. At first, small guns are used. Then larger and larger weapons are fired. The dog slowly learns to adjust to the noise without being afraid.

The obedience course

The obedience course exposes the dog to different situations. Walls, barrels, windows, tunnels, ramps, and steps are used. First the dog walks or crawls through three barrels, each longer than the other. Next, the dog must get through the tunnel. It's more than twelve feet long.

The dog then goes up and down five steps. After the command, "hup," is given, the dog jumps three low

A German shepherd goes through part of the obedience course.

fences. The dog must come to the heel or sit position after each part of the course is finished.

The dog next jumps through a window opening. Then it climbs up and down an A-frame platform that is six feet (1.8 m) high at the center. The dog must then walk across the dogwalk. The dogwalk is like a ladder that is two feet (.6 m) off the ground and nearly nineteen feet (5.8 m) long. A ramp leads on and off on either end.

Special aggressiveness training

The military-patrol dog must be aggressive. But the dog should always be under control. The patrol dog must chase, attack, and hold on to someone on command. The patrol dog must also learn to attack on its own if the handler's life is in danger, or the person (suspect) tries to escape.

Special exercises are used to develop aggressiveness. In the first exercise, a trainer teases the dog with a bag, rag, or arm protector until it bites. The command, ''get him,'' tells the dog to attack. ''Hold him,'' is used when the dog bites. ''Out'' is used to stop the dog's attack. This is practiced again and again until the animal becomes familiar with the commands.

In stand-off training, the escaping suspect will stop running suddenly. The handler calls loudly, ''out,'' then ''heel.'' The dog must stop instantly without attacking.

After three weeks of training, an animal that won't bite is dropped from the program. Some dogs bite, but won't let go. If this can't be corrected, the dog is also dropped. Since the dogs are property of the U.S. government, they cannot be returned to the original owners. Instead, good homes are found for them in the area around Lackland Air Force Base.

Scout training

A dog scouts when it looks for, detects, and warns the handler if a stranger is nearby. At first, the dog and handler stand in a field. The command, ''watch him,'' is given. A person runs and hides behind some bushes.

The handler then gives the command, "find him." The dog moves toward the person. When it gets within fifteen feet, the person gets up and runs. The command "get him" is given. After a short chase, the handler calls the dog off.

In more advanced scouting exercises, the dog detects many well-hidden suspects in different areas. The dog clears the area. This means all people are detected.

Building-search training

A building search lets a dog detect a person in a building by scent, sound, or sight. When the door to the building is opened, the command "find him" is given. When the person is detected, the dog will alert the handler. Sometimes the person tries to escape. The dog is taught to chase and attack. These search exercises are done in different buildings during the day and night.

Tracking

When tracking, the dog follows a person's scent from the ground and from the air near the ground. A short track (or scent trail) is fifty yards. It runs from one point straight to another. At the command "track," the dog starts to follow the scent. An intermediate track is about one hundred yards with two turns. The dog follows the turns and finds cloth, rubber, wool, or leather items left on the track. The handler helps the dog if it loses the track or misses the items.

In an advanced track, the scent turns are sharper. The items are scented with other smells to make it harder for the dog. Sometimes a second track crosses the main track. The advanced track is one to two hours old and about one mile long. Good tracking dogs practice on at least one advanced track a week to keep up their skills.

Some dogs don't want to track. They're not forced to do this special work but, they can stay in the patrol dog program.

Vehicle Patrolling

Some dogs and their handlers have to patrol in a vehicle. Vehicle-patrol training teaches the dog to sit still and not bother the driver or other passengers. The dog jumps into the vehicle only when the command, "hup,"

The Department of Defense Dog Center selects all military dogs for training.

is given. The dog is then commanded to "sit" on the passenger seat.

General information

Military-patrol dogs take about three to four months to learn their skills. But they never quit training. Even experienced dogs are trained four or more hours a week. Practice keeps their skills sharp. Dogs that go more than thirty days without training often have to be retrained.

A military dog may be replaced when it reaches the age of eight years. If the dog is still fit, it may be used to train new handlers at the school.

The value of military dogs

Today, military dogs are useful and effective partners. They give their handlers the added powers of scent, sound, and sight. The dog's sense of smell is forty times better than a person's. They hear twenty times better than people. Dogs can see slight movements at longer distances.

Since 1941, America's military dogs have earned themselves a permanent place in all branches of the armed services. They have proven their value, time and time again, in war and in peacetime.

Glossary

AMBUSH — *Soldiers or people in hiding waiting to make a surprise attack.*

BATTALION — *A large group of soldiers, usually four infantry companies and a headquarters company.*

BOOBY TRAP — *A bomb attached to an every-day object, which explodes if touched or picked up by someone.*

CONTROLLED AGGRESSION — *The patrol dog's ability to work safely around people but still be alert and ready to attack when the handler gives the command.*

DEAD SCENT — *The presence of anything other than a human being (supplies, equipment, other animals) to which trained dogs detect and alert their handlers.*

DISTINGUISHED SERVICE CROSS — *A cross of bronze awarded in the U.S. Army for special heroism in battle.*

HEEL — *The basic command in dog obedience training. The dog walks or sits on the left side of the handler. The dog's right shoulder is in line with the handler's shoulders.*

MASTIFF — *Large, strong, smooth-coated dogs with hanging lips and ears; used in ancient times as attack dogs.*

PURPLE HEART, ORDER OF THE PURPLE HEART — *Started by George Washington as a medal of merit given to U.S. soldiers wounded in action.*

SILVER STAR — *A U.S. military decoration; bronze star with a small silver star at the center, awarded for bravery in action.*

SUPPLY DEPOT — *A place where military supplies and equipment are stored.*

SUSPECT — *A person believed to be acting in a wrong or questionable way; in military dog training, the person whom the dog detects, chases, or attacks.*

TEMPERAMENT — *The emotional characteristics that are special to each dog; its personality or frame of mind.*

TRIP WIRE — *A type of booby trap in which a wire, attached to a bomb, is strung across a trail low to the ground and difficult to see. The bomb explodes when someone or something pushes or walks into it.*

47

*READ ABOUT THE MANY KINDS
OF DOGS THAT WORK FOR A LIVING:*

**HEARING-EAR
DOGS**

**GUIDE
DOGS**

**WATCH/GUARD
DOGS**

**LAW
ENFORCEMENT
DOGS**

**SEARCH
& RESCUE
DOGS**

**STUNT
DOGS**

**SLED
DOGS**

**MILITARY
DOGS**

CRESTWOOD HOUSE